COUNTRY LIVING

Decorating with

Flea Market Finds

from the Editors of Country Living Magazine

foreword by Nancy Mernit Soriano

text by Marie Proeller

Hearst Books, New York

Library of Congress Cataloging-in-Publication Data

Proeller, Marie.
  Decorating with flea market finds / by Marie Proeller and the editors
of Country living.
    p. cm.
  ISBN 1-58816-057-2
    1. House furnishings. 2. Interior decoration 3. Flea markets.
  I. Country living. II. Title.

TX311 .P74 2002
747—dc21   2001039567

Printed in China

First Edition
10 9 8 7 6 5 4 3 2 1
www.countryliving.com

For COUNTRY LIVING
Editor-in-Chief, Nancy Mernit Soriano
Art Director, Susan M. Netzel
Deputy Editor, Lawrence A. Bilotti

Design by Alexis Siroc
Produced by
SMALLWOOD & STEWART, INC.
New York City

contents

foreword

One of the major appeals of country style today is its casual, comfortable approach to decorating: The suitability of mixing old and new. The sense of nostalgia that it imparts. And the personal expression that it affords each of us. Nowhere is this more evident than in flea market decorating, where the search for treasures can transform any room — and accommodate any budget.

In this book, we celebrate the best of flea market decorating by showcasing homes enriched with salvaged building materials, vintage furnishings, and unusual collections, as well as the homeowners for whom the thrill of the hunt — and the discovery of that "great find," with its special memory of time and place — has played an important part in the decorating process.

I hope *Flea Market Finds* inspires you to explore your own personal style and perhaps uncover a "great find" of your own.

Nancy Mernit Soriano

Editor-in-Chief, *Country Living*

introduction

Years ago, interior decorating was a fairly formal affair. Dwellings generally had a set style, showcasing modern designs, for instance, a particular color scheme, or a collection of precious antiques. A young couple moving into their first home purchased matching living-room and bedroom suites; their gleaming sets of china, crystal, and flatware filled cupboards and drawers. Rarely did one combine different looks within a single room setting or shelf-top display. How times change.

Today, a decidedly different, much more exciting home-design trend is sweeping the nation. Inspired by the popularity of our flea markets and the wonderful, one-of-a-kind treasures that we find there, American homeowners are recycling, reusing, and reinventing objects that span centuries, creating a style all their own. We call it "flea market decorating," though the pieces required to achieve the look can be unearthed at a variety of venues: country auctions, yard sales, thrift shops, internet auctions, and the like.

Any number of factors may have contributed to this trend. Some people credit the skyrocketing prices of antiques in the late 1980s followed by the economic slump of the early '90s with sparking the flea-marketing craze in the United States. But as the economy

American homeowners are recycling, reusing, and reinventing flea market objects, creating a style all their own.

enjoyed its steady ascent over the past decade, the popularity of these bazaars did not diminish, but instead grew by leaps and bounds. Obviously there's more afoot here than thrift alone.

From an interior design standpoint, the explanation is simple: Few retail sources offer as wide an array of furniture and accessories representing all eras and interests as do flea markets. Where else can you see weathered farm equipment resting beside a pile of paisley shawls, or a bust of young Elvis preening on a cottage dresser hand-painted with delicate roses? No matter what style speaks loudest to you, whether it's Art Deco, Southwest, or classic country, decorating with flea market finds allows you to create rooms that clearly express who you are and what you love.

An added bonus of this new decorating style is that few rules govern its implementation. Feel like using that painted garden bench as a coffee table? Go right ahead. Want to fill a cookie jar with bath-oil beads and set it next to the tub? Why ever not? All the same, there are basic pointers that will simplify the process. After all, the goal is a uniquely beautiful interior, not a re-creation of an actual flea market. That's where this book comes in. The editors of COUNTRY LIVING have tracked the flea market decorating trend from its earliest beginnings; let us guide you step by step and teach you all you need to know, from spotting a prize amidst a jumble of junk to giving your new possession pride of place in your home.

Our first chapter, **The Flea Market Experience,** examines the allure of the places where one man's trash becomes another man's treasure. In this section you'll also be introduced to some of the most popular collectibles — we call these asides "Flea Classics," and you'll find them throughout the book along with additional snippets on noteworthy decorating and collecting trends. The book's second chapter, **Look Again,** gets to the heart of one of the most important aspects of flea market decorating: Finding new uses for secondhand items. Trade secrets of decorators and stylists will be revealed in **The Art of Display,** a chapter in which we show you how to find the best positions for furniture and accessories throughout the house, whether you're working with single objects, small groupings, or extensive collections.

In our final chapter, **Flea Market Forensics,** you'll find a resource guide unlike any you've seen before. We give you pointers on what to look for (and look out for) in each category — baskets, ceramics, kitchenware, primitive furniture, and toys, to name a few. We also tell you how to prepare for flea market excursions, how to prevail at country or internet auctions, how to beat the antiques dealers to the yard sale bargains, and which corners of thrift shops tend to harbor the most prizes. That certain something you've been searching for can be found once you know where to look; it will shine in your home once you know where to put it.

the flea market experience

Imagine the ultimate treasure hunt and you'll begin to understand the enormous appeal of flea markets. Week after week, at sites across the country, tables are piled high with odds and ends of all descriptions: tangles of Christmas lights, boxes of doorknobs, stacks of old dress patterns. If you don't spot the prize among the pickings, someone else will. Add to this the very atmosphere of flea markets — the buzz of energy from the crowds, the easy camaraderie among the dealers, the excited voice of a shopper who's just spotted her childhood lunch box, the elated expression of a collector who's finally, finally found that elusive pedestal sink — and the continued popularity of these sales becomes even more obvious.

But surely, the uninitiated might venture, the excitement must wane after a dozen or so visits to a particular flea market. Impossible, the aficionado replies. New prizes appear each time dealers unpack their trucks, so you never know what you might find. One

week you may fall in love with a flashy crystal chandelier (the finishing touch the bathroom has always needed), the next week you're scooping up old buttons and beads for a craft project.

True addicts know that the thrill of the hunt extends far beyond the

...the infectious energy of the crowds, the elated expression of a collector who's finally found that elusive pedestal sink...

boundaries of a traditional flea market. Hearing the crack of the auctioneer's gavel as he announces to a packed tent that the blue-painted cupboard on the block is going home with you can set your heart racing just as fast as capturing any flea market bargain, as can the frantic final minutes of an internet auction. Who hasn't gotten a glint in her eye when she spotted a busy yard sale while driving home from the supermarket on a sunny Saturday afternoon? Who hasn't felt a jolt when a teapot of exceptional quality calls out from the clutter? Or suddenly spotted a pristine bedframe lounging against the wall of the thrift shop?

Our urge to uncover special items, especially at bargain prices, is by no means new. In fact, the origins of flea markets date back hundreds of years. Weekly outdoor bazaars held in the small towns of medieval Europe, for example, allowed peasants to sell their produce and craftsmen their wares. As the range of offerings grew to include secondhand household goods, the French dubbed such sales *marchés aux puces*, or, literally, flea markets.

The first European settlers brought the tradition to America, but it wasn't until the beginning of the 20th century that Early

grab it

Nostalgic collectors have exhibited a soft spot for the furniture that once graced the gardens and patios of the mid-1900s. Among the most sought-after is the tubular-steel frame lawn chair—commonly called "a motel chair"—from the 1940s and '50s. Because the chairs were repeatedly exposed to the elements, many display well-worn surfaces; revive the finish with enamel paint.

The sports lover is in: Pegboard mounted on a mud room wall supports vintage sporting goods ranging from canoe paddles and catcher's mitts to boxing gloves and wrestling shoes (opposite). A love of sailing inspired a highly specialized collection of model boats, pond yachts, and other nautical knickknacks (right).

American furniture and folk art first gained widespread popularity among collectors. In this way, the flea markets we adore today — all those stalls brimming with furniture, the rickety tables of bric-a-brac and the odd priceless antique — began their colorful history. In fact, the most acclaimed sales, such as Brimfield in Massachusetts and Lambertville in New Jersey, have been thriving for more than 30 years.

If flea markets have enjoyed centuries of popularity, the penchant to furnish entire rooms — indeed, entire homes — with flea market objects is relatively new. Small wonder that so many people relish the experience — the layering of color and texture, the sense of fun and improvisation, and, perhaps most importantly, the element of surprise. You never know just what you might discover resting around the corner.

flea market country

Brimfield Antique Shows
Brimfield, Massachusetts
May, July & September

Baskets

Baskets are one of the most frequently spotted objects at flea markets. Some may have sustained damage; repair kits come with many different materials and tools for fixing any kind of basket. A large number of the baskets you'll see are new, which does not present a problem if decorative displays are what you've got in mind. Collectors looking for antique and vintage examples, however, should consider these points to avoid baskets of more recent manufacture.

1. Check the price. If it's only a few dollars, chances are good the basket is new.

2. Know your materials. The straps of vintage pack baskets like those from the early 20th century (right) were fashioned from canvas and leather. Some newer designs sport nylon straps.

3. Consider the function. Years ago baskets were made with a particular purpose in mind. Large baskets would have had handles or straps sturdy enough to support significant weights. Newer baskets might have handles in the right places, but close inspection often reveals flimsy construction that would likely break if put to the test.

4. Look for signs of wear. These pieces were put to hard work day after day, so minor repairs and scuffs on corners and rims are commonplace.

5. Ask about age. Be wary of any basket dated 1850s or earlier. Because of the heavy use these items sustained, you'll find few at flea markets that predate the late 1800s. Most vintage examples are from 1900 to 1940.

6. Study construction. As a rule, older baskets display a tighter weave and more intricate detailing than pieces made today.

7. Gently push a splint aside to inspect the color underneath. On older baskets, the protected portion will be lighter than the parts that have been exposed to rain and sun.

Vintage shop signs are always eagerly sought at flea markets, but hand-painted examples are especially desirable (right). Made in the 1940s to hang outside a Pennsylvania general store, the series of signs features vibrant colors on reversible cardboard inserts. Coca-Cola products are the most plentiful soda-pop memorabilia (opposite). As prices for pieces with the red-and-white logo continue to rise, however, interest in other brands like Dr Pepper, RC, Moxie, and Ne-Hi has increased. Reproductions are common at flea markets; some items are clearly marked as new, others are not.

what is it?

Used by fishermen to mark the spot where crab and lobster traps rest underwater, colorful buoys add seaside flair to any interior. Serious collectors seek out painted wooden pieces from the 1920s to the '40s, but even plastic and Styrofoam buoys from the 1950s on are popular today. Age, color, and size are the key factors affecting price. Most buoys stand about 18 inches tall; two-foot examples are rare.

ENJOY
Coca-Cola
DRINK
Coca-Cola
IN BOTTLES
Dr Pepper
DRINK
Coca-Cola
IDEA
FOR
EVERY ME
HOT
COLD
Dr Pepper
frosty
cold!
Dr Pepper

Flower still lifes from the 1930s are the essence of country charm. Some collectors focus on one bloom—roses or pansies are popular—while others try to find as many varieties as possible. Although most of the pieces you'll spot at flea markets were painted by amateurs, many of the same criteria that value fine-art paintings come into play. Color, composition, and degree of detail can all affect the price of a flea market still life, as can the frame that surrounds it. A whimsical border with chipped, weathered paint would be highly prized.

flea market country

Santa Monica Airport Antique & Collectibles Show
Santa Monica, California
Year-round

McCoy Pottery

Although the McCoy Pottery Co., of Roseville, Ohio, was in business for nearly a century, the pieces that most enthusiasts look for today were made in the 1930s and '40s. McCoy was produced in a vast array of colors, sizes, and patterns; some collectors set their sights on one type of object—cookie jars or cornucopia vases—while others focus on a particular color.

More than 20 different marks were used over the years. One of the most common, "NM," for company founder Nelson McCoy, is shown above left. Another frequently spotted symbol is the word "McCoy" over "USA." Some of the earliest McCoy stoneware bears no mark at all (they had paper labels), so people familiar with the weight, glazes, and shapes of these pieces can sometimes find great bargains.

An object's color can greatly affect its desirability. Dealers report that aqua and white are the most popular hues, followed closely by matte green and cobalt blue. McCoy's burgundy glaze has never fared well, and for this reason, pieces bearing the color are often undervalued.

Pattern, too, can affect price. A dark green "beaded" pot is common; a rare aqua "leaf" design would fetch almost three times as much.

Any damage decreases value, whether it is a chip, a crack (sometimes called a "hairline"), or crazing (a web of thin cracks in the glaze). Flaws acquired in manufacturing, such as skips in the glaze, are not considered damages, though they will detract from the most prized pieces.

Graniteware dishpans can be hung on a wall in a decorative display (right) and they can serve as receptacles for ice and beverages at a party. White mixed with blue or gray is the most common combination; white with red, yellow, or green is harder to find. Pristine yellowware bowls can be costly; thrifty collectors build eye-catching displays by scooping up examples with unobtrusive cracks or chips (opposite).

the **history** of kitchenware in the United States is as colorful as it is long, one that is rife with small and large manufacturers constantly trying to outdo each other, introducing gadgets that were lighter in weight, more efficient, or more graphically appealing that those that had come before. Small wonder then that wire whisks, apple parers, egg cups, bread boxes, coffeepots, and the like make up one of the largest categories of objects found at flea markets today. (Yes, even the kitchen sink — especially deep old soapstone models — can be found from time to time.) Among the hottest areas of interest are the artifacts of the first half of the 20th-century kitchen, such as graduated tin canisters, collectible juice glasses, string holders, and enamel-topped tables. Not only are these objects found in abundance, they are also relatively inexpensive, so cheerful groupings are easy to assemble. And they are still functioning — some are downright indestructible.

Mid-1900s juice glasses exhibit a wide array of designs (opposite). Collectors refer to these Mexican motifs as "Fiesta-go-alongs," because they were originally intended to accompany Fiestaware pottery. Vintage syrup pitchers are often chosen to match a kitchen's color scheme (below).

flea market country

Scott Antique Market
Atlanta, Georgia
Year-round

While soft-green Jadeite might be Fire-King's most familiar line, numerous other designs were also produced from the 1940s through the '60s (above). A selection of sought-after pieces is shown here, including a Distlefink mixing bowl with hand-painted red bird and a gold-rimmed platter in Anniversary Rose, a rare pattern produced for only two years during the early '60s. An original lid like the one on a Sealtest Tulip bowl or a label on a square Azurite plate in the Charm pattern, for example, can increase an item's market value.

Depression Glass

During the 1930s and '40s, inexpensive glassware in a rainbow of cheerful hues brightened American kitchens. Manufacturers churned out cups, bowls, pitchers, and plates by the thousands. During the nation's postwar economic boom, Depression glass became a reminder of hard times, and the colorful wares were often discarded or donated to thrift stores by the boxful, creating a deep well today's collectors can tap.

Depression glass collectors tend to focus on a particular color or pattern. The most popular colors are pink and green, although cobalt blue has attracted a strong following as well. As for patterns, some perennial favorites include Cameo, Cherry Blossom, Dogwood, Mayfair, and Miss America.

In addition to color and pattern, certain forms are also prized by collectors—specifically, objects with parts that were easily broken or misplaced, such as handled pitchers, pedestal cake stands, salt-and-pepper shaker sets, and covered candy dishes, cookie jars, refrigerator containers, and sugar bowls. Combine a desirable form with a rare pattern—like the Poinsettia pitcher shown above left—and the result is extremely valuable.

Reproductions of some of the more popular Depression-glass patterns are not uncommon. Be wary of designs that look too crisp and objects that appear unused. Remember, families dined with these pieces day after day; a plate or bowl that seems to have survived without any visible signs of wear and tear should raise eyebrows.

Monogrammed sheets and tablecloths with minimal repairs and
staining can bring premium prices
in the marketplace (opposite).
Some collectors look for their
own initials, while others purchase
whatever they can find. Displayed
on open shelves, the elegant
detailing can be appreciated by
owner and guests alike. Charming
vintage dress trimmings are rarely
found in full skeins, but even
remnants are scooped up when
they surface (right).

household linens are

another flea market staple. From the

most humble printed tablecloth to the

most exquisite doily edged with hand-

made lace, there's something about the textures, colors, patterns, and details of

these items that continues to win over new devotees year after year. This is also

an area of collecting in which many dealers specialize. Befriend the linen vendors

at your local flea market and chances are good that they will keep an eye out for

your favorite things while on buying runs and set them aside for you.

Vintage fabrics in particular have become wildly popular recently, not

only among people looking to reupholster furniture or make curtains, but also

among craftspeople, who use the colorful prints to make pillows, skirts, and tote

bags. The more yardage there is available in a particular pattern, and the more

pristine its condition, the more valuable the fabric will be.

Delicate linen hankies usually cost no more than a dollar apiece (right); more costly exceptions include souvenirs of popular travel destinations or events like the World's Fair. Floral fabric patterns from the 1940s have timeless appeal (opposite). Color schemes range from soft pastels like these to tropical blooms in bold ochre, teal, and maroon.

Original paper labels are desirable, generally indicating that a handkerchief, tablecloth, or tea towel has never been used or even laundered. Those collectors who wish to put their new possessions to use, however, have been known to remove the tags; those who plan to incorporate the textiles into displays most often take care to leave labels in place.

If linens display the yellowing of age or discoloration along fold lines, soak them overnight in cool water mixed with white vinegar or a detergent like Biz. All but the most fragile pieces can then be washed in the gentle cycle. For stubborn stains, try a paste of white vinegar and salt, or dab some lemon juice on the spot and lay the piece in the sun. Once laundered, hang linens on a clothesline, then press with a warm iron while they're still slightly damp. Avoid dry cleaning, as the harsh chemicals can sometimes damage vintage textiles.

State Tablecloths

Among the most desirable items today are colorful printed-cotton tablecloths bearing the popular sights of a particular state. Because demand for these textiles is strong, they are usually priced slightly higher than everyday cotton tablecloths bearing fruit or flowers.

The most common tablecloths on the market hail from the states that saw the greatest tourist traffic over the years, including California, Florida, Arizona, Massachusetts, and New Jersey. Examples from popular destinations within a state, like Niagara Falls, the Grand Canyon, Atlantic City, or Hollywood are also abundant.

Souvenirs from less-traveled parts of the country like Alaska, Nebraska, or North Dakota are more difficult to find and cost more. For this reason, building a specialized collection with examples from each of the 50 states can be a challenge.

Some designs were offered with four matching napkins; keep an eye out for complete sets, which are considered a real find for collectors.

In general, fans of these textiles focus on a region for which they feel a personal connection. Someone with a vacation home in Florida, for instance, might devote their search to that state alone, while a couple who honeymooned on Cape Cod would have a soft spot for that motif. Many collectors also seek out tablecloths from their friends' home states, as these pieces make meaningful gifts for birthdays, bridal showers, and housewarmings.

look again

One of the greatest joys — and greatest challenges — of flea market decorating is finding a castoff from another time and place that can begin a new life as something entirely different. Leave your notions about what things are *supposed* to be at home. Instead, look at objects in a vendor's stall as if they'd just fallen to earth. Your eye sees a nice, fat rusted wire clam basket; your brain might tell you it's a hearth-side container for kindling; your heart might say its fate is to be spray-painted and filled with magazines or stationed in the mudroom to collect the children's rain boots. Perhaps it could be lined with white canvas and relocated to the sitting room, filled with fuzzy balls of yarn and knitting needles. Or should it become a seasonal decoration, planted with snappy geraniums for summer, inhabited by pinecones all winter? But wait — how about lining it with plastic to hold ice and bottles of soda, wine, and beer at your parties?

The gratification that comes with decorating like this appeals to people who feel better knowing that instead of buying brand-new objects, they are preserving — and recycling — parts of the past. Others love the design possibilities: How can we create a bookshelf with salvaged materials? Could that dresser become a vanity for the sink in the new bathroom? Would the pie safe work as a cabinet for my collection of vases? Then there are people who will tell you that they just prefer the quality of second-hand furnishings to that of the goods available on the retail market. Indeed, the majority of tables, dressers, and cupboards made up until the mid-20th century are strong, well-constructed pieces of fine quality woods.

flea market country

Kane County Flea Market
St. Charles, Illinois
Year-round

Sometimes the object you discover can move right into your home with minimal fuss, needing only a quick laundering or a fresh coat of paint to prepare it for its new life. Other pieces may require substantial repairs or alterations, like sawing an opening

Knowing that you're giving new life to something from the past is part of the appeal of flea market shopping.

in the top of a dresser for a sink. Investing in these repairs almost always repays you handsomely, with years of service.

When you're hunting about at the flea market, think of creative solutions to glaring problems: Of course a sideboard can be a bedroom dresser — its compartmentalized silverware drawer just begs to hold socks. A glass-front cabinet doesn't have to be in the dining room: It will work beautifully in the bathroom, with family toiletries, or in the pantry, holding canned goods, or in the sewing room, filled with fabrics and trims. Little step stools make wonderful display stands for pottery and plants. Position an old porcelain tray behind the kitchen sink faucets — a beautiful back-splash. Stains on part of an exquisite damask tablecloth? Make the pristine parts into pillowcases. That's the fun of it all.

Ingenious ideas abound in a Maryland living room. To make the coffee table, an 1880s playpen was flipped over and topped with a marble slab. The chaise longue, now with soft feather pillows, was originally for outdoor use. On the mantel, revamped kerosene lamps flank an 1890s weathervane. The dramatic iron candelabra were used for garden weddings. An architectural column with an ornate top adds visual height to the low-ceilinged space.

Plentiful, comfortable seating is so important in the living room. Fortunately, flea markets offer up endless possibilities. It is always possible to find a matching sofa, love seat, and armchair suite in great condition. More often, however, homeowners unify individual pieces by having them reupholstered or slipcovered with a single fabric pattern, or two complementary patterns. You can also supplement the living-room furniture you've had for years with additional types of seating like generous ottomans at the foot of wing chairs and slipper chairs flanking a secretary, bookcase, or hearth.

Broaden your search to include not only traditional choices but also unexpected items like garden furnishings — Adirondack chairs, wrought-iron patio sets, and rustic benches. Consider objects originally designed for other rooms in the house. Victorian iron cribs, for example, can be transformed into charming love seats by removing one side of the frame and adding an upholstered cushion. Twin-size cast-iron beds piled with fat pillows make cozy daybeds. A collection of

Garden trellises add a graphic element to a serene setting (opposite). A painted workshop bench provides just enough space in front of the sofa for a fruit bowl and a stack of coffee table books. Leaning against a wall, an elegant mirror makes a room appear larger (right). The fan-shaped fireplace screen was salvaged from an old bank in Pennsylvania.

kitchen stepladders or library ladders can lend graphic interest and provide extra seating in a pinch.

Televisions, VCRs, and stereos:

Keep them out of sight in an elegant armoire or a country cupboard you have converted for just this purpose. Small blanket chests and trunks can do double duty as coffee tables and storage space for playing cards, coasters, videos, remote controls, and other living-room miscellany; apothecary chests with dozens of tiny drawers can organize your everyday necessities in style. Set beside the sofa, a weathered wheelbarrow holds books and magazines; the same garden accessory positioned beneath a window might be home to an attractive arrangement of potted flowering bulbs.

flea market country

Starway Flea Market
Wilmington, North Carolina
Year-round

Mirrors

The world's first mirrors were actually polished sheets of metal. It wasn't until the early 1500s that artisans in Italy's famed Murano glassworks invented true mirrors by applying a thin reflective foil to panes of clear glass. Most antique mirrors found at flea markets today date from the mid-1800s through the early 1900s.

1. Inspect the glass. Antique glass is rarely in perfect condition, but commonly displays an overall grayness and small black spots where the backing has come off.

2. Frames tell a story. Most country mirrors are surrounded by simple wood frames; mirrors that hung in more affluent homes often feature ornate gilded frames. Whether they are simple or opulent, antique frames should show signs of age.

3. Turn the mirror over. Many antique examples have brown-paper backing; if the paper is original to the frame, it should exhibit some flaking at the corners and occasional staining.

4. Do screws, nails, and wire appear to be from the same period as the glass and frame?

5. Is the price right? Because these pieces are considered antiques rather than simply household accessories, they often carry heftier price tags than new mirrors.

6. Ask about provenance. Can the dealer tell you where he or she found the piece? Did it come out of an estate sale or is it known to have hung in a 19th-century barbershop?

7. Don't pass on framed pieces with broken glass. Period replacement glass can often be tracked down through architectural-salvage sources and at other flea markets. Mirrors with crackling around the edges can be cut down to fit a smaller frame.

Remnants of a chenille pom-pom bedspread brought new life to whitewashed vintage stools (right). In the fireplace, a grouping of pillar candles set on an ironstone platter provides an unexpected alternative to traditional logs. The addition of vintage mirrored glass and small, semicircular shelves transformed a pair of panel doors into architectural plant stands (opposite). The legs of an old harvest table were shortened to make the coffee table; pressed-tin tiles adhered to a small crate create an eye-catching center-piece. A button-front gingham dress lends a sense of humor to a graceful but discarded side chair.

one-note collector

Many hat stand collections begin as natural—and practical—extensions of vintage hat collections. Flea markets are ideal places to search for these pieces, which were made in a dizzying array of styles, including some with papier-mâché heads. Among the most popular designs with collectors today are 1950s painted wood stands.

VENICE

NANTUCKET
ROBERT GAMBEE

SIPADAN

CHESAPEAKE COUNTRY

GARDENS OF MEXICO

GARDENS IN PROVENCE

the house of the architect

Nantucket Island   Robert Gambee

SALGADO WORKERS APERTURE

THE SPLENDOR OF FRANCE
Great Châteaux, Mansions, and Country Houses
MEDITERRANEAN VERNACULAR

WORLD'S MOST BEAUTIFUL SEASHELLS

Filling large expanses of wall space can be tricky; one home-owner solved the problem with an arched window salvaged from an Ohio church (opposite). A diminutive upholstered footstool serves as a small coffee table in front of the iron-framed daybed, which has been dressed with a Victorian drapery panel. A pair of weathered barn doors accented with an amateur oil painting brings interest to another living room wall (above). Salvaged columns serve as pedestals for decoys and other small sculptures.

flea market country

Buchanan's Antiques & Collectibles Flea Market
Oklahoma City, Oklahoma
Year-round

FLEA MARKET ROOM

The Palette

White brings calm to a living room and gives the space an open, airy feeling. Echo colors in walls, window treatments, and upholstery fabric.

Upholstery Options

Slipcovers made from a single fabric unify mismatched sofas and chairs. Easy-care covers are practical for families with kids and pets.

Salvaged Mantels

An antique mantel gives a room instant personality. Leave chipping paint or strip and repaint the mantel to match existing woodwork.

Surfaces

A wide farm table stands behind the sofa, a blanket chest is a coffee table (and storage), and a garden bench supports plants at the window.

Nontraditional Artwork

Try a weathervane, tavern sign, or an architectural element over the mantel. A length of Victorian millwork can echo a mantel's lines.

Accessories

Use some decorative elements as they were intended, like candlesticks on a mantel. Give some new purpose; old buckets are pretty cachepots.

Whimsical lamp bases can be created out of any number of flea market finds, like a baluster from an old staircase (right). Talk about adapt and reuse: An entire structure was reclaimed by its owners (opposite). Formerly a poultry house, the space was thoroughly scrubbed and white-washed before playful touches like the child's wagon filled with Bauer pottery bowls were added. Vintage birdcages, bird prints, and embroidered bird pillows pay homage to the room's original ornithological occupants.

just as good

Made for myriad kitchen duties over the centuries, wire baskets have never out-grown their usefulness. On a countertop, they hold onions, potatoes, or apples just as well as they ever did. The charming pieces can be toted to the vegetable patch to bring back fresh tomatoes, peppers, radishes, or whatever harvest the garden may yield.

Spectacular arched windows suspended from antique chains create a transparent boundary between living room and home office areas. A canvas floorcloth distinguishes the office from the parquet in the rest of the house. Quirky collections inspire creative thoughts in the airy space. An antique school desk is the catwalk for a blowsy dress-maker's mannequin; the wire clam basket beneath the desk now catches wastepaper. Buckets and florist vases are inverted and stacked on top of one another to add height as well as visual interest to the display.

flea market country

Elephant's Trunk Bazaar
New Milford, Connecticut
March to December

A farmhouse dining room is host to a family of chairs adopted from living room, den, and office (opposite). A coat of aqua paint transformed four oak office chairs from the early 1900s into seating in a sunny breakfast nook (right). From a shelf above the windows, aqua and yellowware bowls mirror the room's color scheme.

**ollow your heart** when you design your dining room: Shield-back side chairs and wedding-band china are timeless choices, no doubt about it, but if blue-painted pie chests and Fiestaware are more attractive to you, indulge yourself. Weathered kitchen farm tables are favorites in dining rooms that can accommodate their length; if you're hosting a formal dinner, cover the top with a vintage banquet cloth. Ample seating is another priority for a space in which guests want to linger. Matching sets of six or eight chairs are eagerly sought and rarely last long in a dealer's booth. If a chair search proves fruitless, unify assorted models with a single color of paint. Picnic benches, too, can replace conventional side chairs. Let a Hoosier cupboard or open shelving house china, flatware, and glassware collections. The room's finishing touch? Anything you like — a doll collection, a piece of folk art, or an enormous transferware platter.

Wooden cutlery carriers were common in Early-American homes (opposite). When used in their traditional manner, the sturdy pieces make setting the table a breeze, indoors or out. Some found on the market today are simply varnished; others are painted in solid shades of blue, red, or cream.

The carrier's simple form lends itself to countless interpretations (left and above). Set on a desktop, one can organize office supplies (tiny flowerpots might hold paper clips, rubber bands, and other items). Personal collections like seashells, glass ornaments, even baseball cards stand out when arranged in the versatile containers.

The Table

Find a table that suits the style of
your dining activities. Patio tables
are light and airy, and their glass
tops are easy to keep clean.

Seating Solutions

Match the chairs or, since sets
are scarce, choose designs that
share balance and basic style and
harmonize them with color.

Space for Storage

Roomy antique cupboards,
dressers, even medicine cabinets,
can house plates, serving pieces,
glasses, linens, and more.

Lighting

A ceiling fixture can be the most
fun in the dining room. Fit it with
soft candlelight bulbs and decorate
it with flowers or vines.

Dining Details

Invite drama or whimsy. Folding
screens, fat potted plants, and a few
quirky collections can be rotated
for seasonal change.

The Centerpiece

Fruit bowls, pottery consoles
and candleholders are flea market
classics; so are candelabra,
garden urns, and wood troughs.

What could be simpler? Strips of muslin stand in for missing hardware on a chest of drawers (right). Irish pudding bowls in various sizes serve everything from cereal to ice cream. Sap buckets, flattened to lie flat and strung with wire, make a colorful display along a dining-room wall (opposite). Cut-out words hint at some of the new jobs the vintage pieces can take on, like holding letters or dried herbs and flowers.

just as good

While many vintage chandeliers and lamps need only to be plugged in, others will require rewiring. Do-it-yourselfers with basic electrical skills can visit a hardware store for supplies and consult a home-repair book for instructions; less handy folks should give the piece to an electrician or bring it to a repair shop.

Weathered iron feed bins can hold bushels of apples, potatoes, or onions (below). Before eating produce that's been stored in them, wash off any rust that might have flaked onto the food. The bins also help organize garden tools, flowerpots, and all those items destined for recycling.

An old milking stool is reborn as a dish rack at a pristine vintage kitchen sink (above). The doors to the wall cupboards were removed to create open shelving. Branches of fall bittersweet brighten an antique wooden box (opposite). Beside the box, a tassel-shaped iron weight from the 19th-century adds a sculptural touch to the tabletop arrangement.

To create a distinctive bed skirt, printed handkerchiefs were attached to a cotton panel with fusible tape. For a comfortable headboard, a plywood plank was padded with polyester batting and a matelassé coverlet was tacked around it. Flower-filled canning jars arranged along simple painted wood shelves add an extra dash of color to the room.

as the bed is the heart of any room it occupies, the bed frame you choose sets the tone for the rest of the room. Sleigh beds, for example, have a formal feel to them, perhaps inspiring a selection of mahogany furniture and damask fabrics throughout the space. A whitewashed iron frame, on the other hand, would complement hand-painted cottage dressers and sheer, breezy fabrics.

Flea markets basically offer two options: traditional designs (iron beds, sleigh beds, four-posters, canopies) and original interpretations fashioned from heavy vintage doors, fencing, barn wood, old columns, and other salvaged materials.

Sometimes, finding the bed of your dreams requires some creative vision. If you spot the exact piece you've been searching for — an early-1900s pale blue wood frame with graceful acorn finials — but you realize it's a twin bed and you need a queen: Fear not. Skilled carpenters can easily widen a frame by sawing the head and foot

flea market country

Princeton Flea Market
Princeton, Wisconsin
April to August

A graceful garden chair and an architectural star supply the decorative elements in a peaceful setting (opposite). In another bedroom, a metal stool acts as a nightstand, while a sap bucket stands ready as a wastebasket (right). The bed's headboard was wrapped with blue-and-white ticking fabric. Framed postcards, an office clock, and an old shelf enliven the wall.

boards down the center, adding strips of wood that follow the lines of the original design, and applying a fresh coat of paint to mask old and new parts. For 19th-century rope beds and other antique frames you wouldn't dare cut in two, lay a plywood plank cut to fit across the frame and top it with a full-size futon. Mask the soft edges of the futon with a plump duvet. Headboards can be created from any number of items — sideboard mirrors, oversized frames and artwork, painted shutters.

Supplement closet space with roomy armoires or cupboards fitted with shelves and clothing racks. Blanket chests set at the foot of the bed can keep sweaters and woolen blankets safe throughout the year when they are scented with natural moth repellents like lavender sachets. And small containers such as hatboxes, wicker baskets, and wooden cutlery cases are ideal for artfully stashing toiletries, jewelry, and sewing supplies.

A portion of metal balcony railing discovered at a junkyard became a graphic headboard in a pared-down bedroom. The built-in ledge that supports the railing doubles as a bookshelf. Mid-20th-century card catalogues flank the bed, holding all manner of nightstand necessities such as tissues, paperbacks, and reading glasses. On the table beside the window, a kitchen ceiling light has been converted into a lamp and a chemistry beaker holds two curvaceous feathers.

flea market country

Annex Antiques Sale & Flea Market
New York City, New York
Year-round

Can't find the bed frame that's right for you? One creative homeowner designed her own with salvaged architectural fragments (right). A painted bench set beneath the window affords its sitter sweeping garden views. Because there wasn't enough spare wall space in another room to position a king-size bed, the homeowner constructed a free-standing headboard (opposite). Adorned with tin ceiling tiles and a transom window, the hollow headboard contains spacious shelving and clothes racks that are accessible from the other side.

what to do?

As you wander the aisles of a flea market, you're sure to spot the occasional glass vessel that has lost its lid. Don't pass it by. These pieces are usually inexpensive (the serious collectors prefer all original parts intact), and they make sweet informal vases for tables and windowsills. Many are beautifully etched and delicately shaped and, who knows, you may find a lid to fit at another flea market.

Architectural Salvage

Although people restoring old houses have long relied on salvaged doors, windows, and floorboards to bring period authenticity to their projects, thinking of architectural fragments as decorative elements is a relatively recent phenomenon.

One of the most popular ways to display these pieces is to hang a single section of wrought-iron fence, tin ceiling tile, or a carved wood panel (right) on the wall, drawing attention to sculptural qualities that might otherwise go unnoticed.

Witty interpretations of the trend can be devised as well. Try placing unexpected objects over a doorway, such as a portico (opposite) saved from the demolition of an Iowa farmhouse, or building a bed frame with portions of picket fence.

Freestanding pieces like those fabulous old brownstone and cement gargoyles make terrific tabletop sculptures and doorstops.

Architectural fragments also serve practical purposes. Columns can become pedestals; squat sections make wonderful side tables. Solid old doors are great tabletops and headboards, and battered weathervanes look even better in the smaller proportions of a room.

Because many dealers bring only prime examples of architectural salvage to a flea market, junkyards are good places to hunt for bargains. Toss a flashlight and a pair of work gloves into your bag before you go there.

Ceramic canisters from the kitchen are reassigned to a vanity to make ideal storage for earrings and toiletries (opposite). A small garden urn painted white to match the rest of the collection is filled with blazing-colored marigolds. Also from the kitchen, a trio of ironstone pitchers and a striped English pudding bowl rest on a whitewashed cottage dresser (right).

did your grandmother

keep buttons in brightly colored coffee

cans? Then you know that thinking up

practical uses for decorative accessories combines the best of both worlds. Kitchen

canisters — whether from a graduated set or commercial containers

for coffee, biscuits, or pretzels — are natural choices for this

type of reinvention. Imagine, in a craft room, spare open

shelves lined with colorful tins holding beads, notions,

fabric remnants, and snippets of ribbon. To spark ideas

for placement and purpose, analyze an object's form and

flea market country

Lambertville Antiques Market
Lambertville, New Jersey
Year-round

function. Ceramic pitchers, glass milk bottles, and canning jars, for

example, make natural receptacles for garden flowers, while wooden boxes that

long ago held seed packets in the general store can accommodate stationery

supplies in a home office or toiletries on a dresser.

Linen

The timeless beauty of real linen is undeniable. Yet it can sometimes be difficult to tell if a vintage tea towel is linen or cotton, or perhaps a blend of the two. With their years of experience, fabric experts have a sixth sense when it comes to such matters. Here, they offer hints for spotting the real thing:

1. Closely examine the weave. Tea towels of linen, for instance, often display a larger, irregular weave when compared to cotton or linen-cotton blends.

2. Look for labels. Unused items may retain their original paper labels; laundered pieces sometimes feature a small cloth tab along the bottom edge.

3. Clutch the fabric in your hand. Press tightly and hold it for a few seconds. If the piece creases heavily in just a short time, it's most likely linen.

4. Hold never-washed pieces up to the light. While linen gets softer with each wash, household items that have remained in storage will have a noticeable sheen to them.

5. Has a tablecloth been starched? If so, chances are good that it's linen. Homemakers rarely took such trouble with the cotton tablecloths employed for more casual meals.

6. Seek out sheets made in the 1920s or '30s, when much of the everyday bedding available in department stores was pure linen.

7. Is there a patina of age on a piece of antique homespun linen? Be wary of new linen blends that lack the mellowness that comes with repeated use.

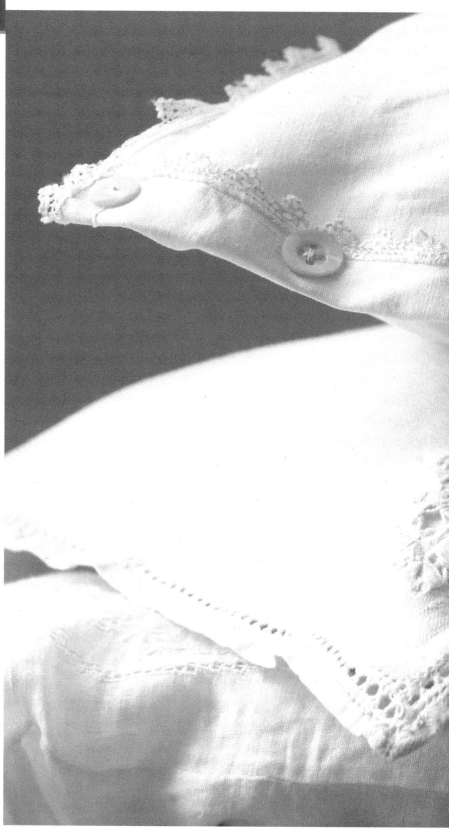

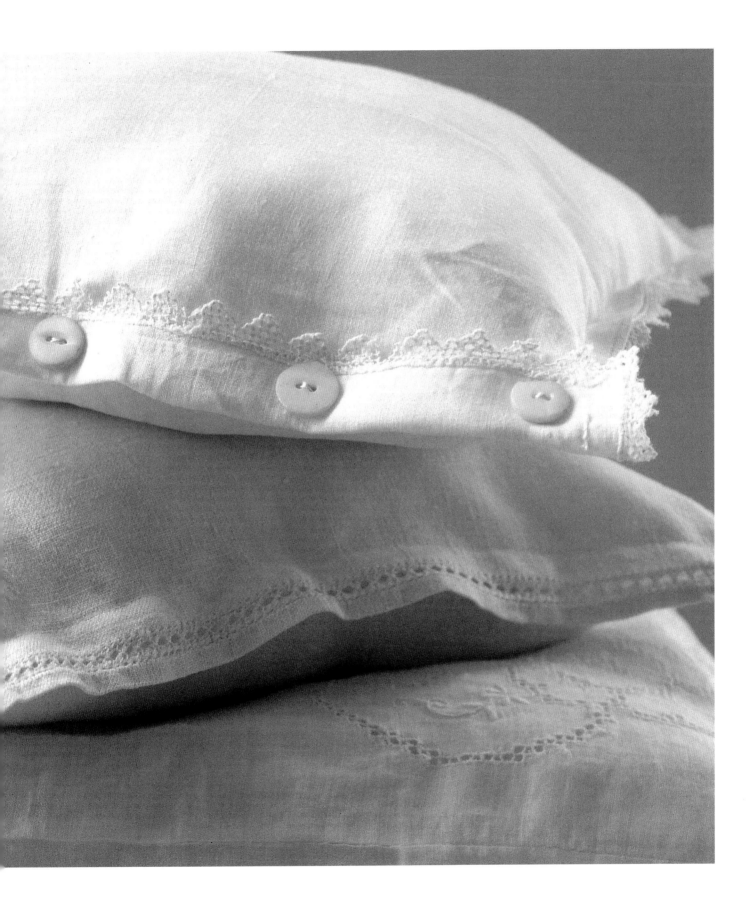

Because condition affects the price of vintage textiles, table-cloths and napkins with significant stains or damage can often be scooped up for a few dollars each. The remnants can make colorful pillows (above). A piece of a chenille pom-pom bedspread backs the graphic rose print. Pearly buttons add texture and shimmer to the checkered napkin.

Remnant Chic

There are almost as many uses for vintage fabrics as there are patterns on the market. Florals, stripes, checks, polka dots—whatever design catches your eye, you can turn it into something terrific. Only a decade ago, tattered tablecloths and bolts of upholstery fabric were practically worthless. Today they are prominently displayed on dealers' tables.

Creative folks regularly snatch up the remnants for tote bags, pillow shams, kitchen curtains, fabric-wrapped frames and photo albums, potholders, and eyeglass cases. Dressmakers even tailor jackets, dresses, and skirts with vintage fabrics and table linens.

Fabric scraps can serve as mats under frames, coverings for pin cushions, and tea cozies. Larger pieces make distinctive lampshades.

When shopping for fabric, expand your search to include unfinished quilt tops and individual squares, mattress ticking, old cotton housedresses and aprons, men's worsted suits and silk ties. Many companies make reproduction fabric as well, which some craftspeople choose when a project needs extra strength, like handles on tote bags.

Always wash vintage fabrics when you get them home, then fold and stack them in a cupboard or on a shelf. Many people sort them by color or by theme (fruit, flowers, or animals, for example). Others arrange their collections by material—cotton, linen, silk, wool, and so on.

To create a shower curtain, a chenille bedspread was lined and reinforced along the top (right). An exquisitely embroidered linen table runner hangs at the window. Twin sinks and a galvanized metal top transformed a farm table into a dual vanity (opposite). The medicine cabinets were painted the same color and scuffed to imitate age.

Whether you're looking to outfit the tiniest powder room or the most luxurious master bath, flea market finds can serve in countless ways. Glass apothecary and barber-shop jars provide transparent storage for Band-Aids, cotton balls, and bath-oil beads; wicker baskets in various sizes keep towels accessible; and colorful ceramic planters hold fragrant potpourris or miniature hand soaps. If you spot a bolt of vintage fabric you adore, consider incorporating it into the bath, where both lively patterns and solid colors can be transformed into shower curtains, window treatments, and sink skirts. Whimseys, too, can happily exist in a bathroom. Look for birdhouses, vintage enamelware signs, gazing balls, garden statues, architectural fragments — anything that won't be damaged by humidity but does strike your fancy.

flea market country

Florida Twin Markets
Mt. Dora, Florida
Year-round

Vintage Tubs

These elegant pieces are common sights at salvage yards; a new porcelain finish—in any color —makes them shine like new.

New Fittings

In many cases, you can even find the same style of brass or chrome that would have outfitted the piece in its original setting.

Privacy

In a generously proportioned bath, salvaged doors can be hinged together to create a folding screen around the tub or commode.

New Purpose

A metal garden chair makes a fine towel rack in the bathroom. A metal trunk beneath the sink replaces the medicine cabinet.

Themes

Vintage outdoor light fixtures hang on the wall behind the bathtub; architectural columns brace a wall-hung sink.

Balance

If the furnishings are bold, balance the look with a neutral color scheme. Let brighter color enliven rooms with more delicate details.

APOTHEC

In a bathroom with a skylight, an old potting table holds the sink (opposite). An antique hanging cupboard acts as a medicine cabinet, while a wooden bucket becomes a wastebasket. Plush towels are stored on the open shelf; a supply of washcloths is kept nearby in a wooden cutlery carrier. The apothecary sign on the wall dates to the late 1800s. In one gardener's bathroom, the walls and tub enclosure were sheathed in chicken wire so that a clinging vine could thrive in the setting (right). An old suitcase beside the tub supports a small bucket filled with soap, a sea sponge, and a loofah. The sink skirt and shower curtain were sewn from vintage linen.

grab it

Victorian garden urns are in demand! Collectors admire the cast-iron pieces for their ornate designs and their versatility around the house. Whether it is hand towels in the powder room, lemons in the kitchen, or fresh flowers just about anywhere, everything seems more elegant in these virtually indestructible containers. Size and condition affect price; handled examples are especially prized.

the art of display

Every object tells a story. When you look at a beloved bowl or painting or pie chest, you will remember where you found it, whom you were with, and how much you bargained over it. But when that object gets lost in a crowded arrangement, your sense of enjoyment is somewhat diminished. If, on the other hand, it is settled where your eye can fall on it throughout the day, your gratification increases all the more. And surely that's the point.

The art of display is focusing attention on important pieces and makes great collections look even better. The first lesson is to learn how to analyze the layout of a room. Is there one large area of wall space or a long, bare table that the eye is immediately drawn to? If so, concentrate your energy on that area. Next, consider your collections themselves. What type of object would make that space look finished? A single graphic sign or a selection of photographs or prints might enliven the empty wall, while a cluster of colored-glass

vases concentrated at the center of the table would add a punch of color.

One primary rule of display is "Like with Like": The common element of a collection can be its color (anything that's green); its substance (ruby glass of all kinds); its theme (anything remotely roses); its imprimatur (a mix of Floraline pottery). Create various arrangements with articles that relate to each other. Your flock of wooden duck decoys deserves a roost together, perhaps on a mantel. Souvenir plates always look best together, set along a shelf or hung on the wall. Don't hesitate to toss in an oddball yet oddly related piece: for instance, those decoys might take comfort alongside a roomy birdhouse. If you are arranging delicate pieces, consider the security of a glass-front curio cabinet.

What about all those small objects — silver baby cups, velvet pincushions, old medicine bottles, antique fountain pens —

that somehow seem to get lost in the mix? Dedicate a hanging cupboard or wall shelf to only those items.

The actual arrangement of objects will often depend on the prevailing style in a room. If a space has a minimalist feeling, collections generally look best when pared down and precisely

Every object tells a story, if you let it.

arranged — airy rows of white ironstone pitchers in a cupboard, for instance, or matching urns placed at either end of a mantel. In rooms that are a riot of color and pattern, placement can have a more casual look. Why not line the tops of the kitchen cupboards with pitchers of all colors, sizes, and materials, or push both urns to one side of the mantel, fill them with Queen Anne's lace, and stack vintage gardening books on the other end?

Remember, direct sunlight can dramatically fade prints, photographs, vintage textiles, and painted finishes, so take care to avoid window-side placement

flea market country

Springfield Antique Show & Flea Market
Springfield, Ohio
Year-round

of these pieces. Because temperature and humidity fluctuations affect furniture and accessories alike, position cherished pieces far from radiators, heating vents, and air conditioners.

A keen gardener conjures up his own distinctive way to greet guests in his front hall and staircase. Miniature topiaries and a collection of vintage lawn sprinklers lining the steps whimsically announce his hobby. Antique gilt-framed mirrors reflect sunlight and garden views while lending a touch of finery to the botanical displays.

Whether it's spacious or not, an entry can do more than admit family and friends to the house. It's your first opportunity to state who you are and what your home is like — and to have some decorating fun. We stand in, then walk through, entries, so walls become gallery spaces for anything we care to display. Rather than hanging a large-scale vintage map over the couch in the living room, hang it up in the hall, where people can get close and scrutinize it.

If your passion is blue-and-white transferware, hang plates and platters from your collection like a frieze at the tops of the walls, or center just one on either side of a mirror. If you love the theater, line the walls with identically framed playbills, advertising posters, and newspaper reviews. Look for items that invite inspection — intricately woven textiles, group photographs from an old summer camp, carved tramp art frames — anything that will serve as an introduction to your home, and will become terrific conversation pieces in the bargain. Then just be sure to have wonderful overhead lighting, so everything can be admired.

The old adage "less is more" does not hold sway in many country interiors. The owner of one collection-filled home, for instance, follows quite a different rule (opposite). In the entrance hall, panoramic photographs from the early to mid-1900s monopolize wall space, while terra-cotta medallions punctuate the simple silhouette of the steps. On a garden-lover's desk, bird's nests, flowerpots, and terra-cotta border tiles combine to create a memorable landscape (right). A glass fly-catcher hangs from a drawer pull.

what is it?

Glass fly-catchers, filled with a bit of sugar water and corked on top, were set on windowsills and hung from trees to keep pests away from people and gardens. The flies were lured into the openings at the bottoms and would be unable to find their way out again. Three examples include a footed model from the late 1800s and two wire-topped 1930s pieces.

Arranging a Shelf

On a well-designed shelf, every object is enhanced by the others, and each takes on added resonance because of its companions.

Shelf arrangements can be beautiful whether they are precisely spaced identical items or a mixture of loosely related objects. Their selection and place-ment create the balance that makes them work.

Consider, first, the style of the room. If it's pared-down, a single line of similar objects—leather-bound books or ironstone pitchers, for example—may be the best way to go. On the other hand, if you believe the more the merrier, pile on objects and materials to your heart's content.

For layered arrangements, set your foundations first, then place accessories around them. Move around major pieces like books, engravings, and urns to establish the foundation; fill out the arrangement with smaller figurines, framed snap-shots, and other whimsical items.

An element of nature enlives any shelf display, from a single rose in a bud vase to a bowl of apples to a stately snake plant.

Once you achieve an arrangement you like, don't be afraid to shake it up and rethink it periodically. That's the fun of it.

A sense of ease wafts through a vacation home, where the family's love of antiques and the great outdoors is evident in the objects they surround themselves with. Among the room's treasures are a handmade pond yacht on the mantel, a wooden Canada goose "stick-up," and a green tool caddie filled with volumes about geography and natural history.

as the main gathering place, the living room is an ideal space to display collections. You may not even know that you are a collector, but veteran flea marketers consider "two of anything" the beginning of a collection. Perhaps you're attracted to landscape paintings — hang them all together in the living room. Paint-by-numbers pieces are exceptionally popular too. If you have travel photos of faraway

Collections spark conversation among your guests.

places, mount them on the wall and stack old suitcases beside the sofa. Think beyond the walls: Mantels are a focal point in the living room, so grace yours with the most eye-catching objects in a collection. Long banks of bookshelves look best when a vase or small sculpture allows visual relief from spine after spine of volumes. And coffee tables are sensible repositories for the kinds of objects that can be picked up and looked over — snowglobes, tin toys, marble eggs.

When a collection is made up of small items, it's easy to contain it within a cabinet or along a shelf. With larger objects—like architectural models and vintage birdhouses—another approach is called for. Placed in various spots throughout the room, the weathered wood forms have enough space to be appreciated on their own and also coax the eye to move from object to object. Unframed oil-on-canvas landscapes complement the room's casual atmosphere.

flea market country

Big Pevely Flea Market
Pevely, Missouri
Year-round

Place a cherished object far off the beaten path, alongside a stair landing, for instance, like a birdhouse on a garden bench (right), where it will give guests a pleasant surprise when they happen upon it. Another option is to make fragile pieces, like a majestic church-steeple bird-house, the focal point of a room (opposite). A structure's sculptural qualities stand out when it's placed in the center of a narrow farm table in a sunroom. The home's bare, four-pane windows and a row of painted plank-seat chairs reinforce the strong, simple lines of the birdhouse.

what is it?

To provide attractive support, a cast-iron star was attached to the outside of a brick wall, capping an interior rod. By and large, antique examples are rarely found in large quantities. New ones, priced at only a few dollars each, are an affordable alternative to period pieces. Dealers specializing in architectural salvage are the best sources for the real thing.

Themes

Arranging by theme has long been popular with homeowners and decorators who realize that showcasing similar items heightens a collection's impact. Having a favorite subject to search for also makes flea market shopping more fun.

An object's size can affect its placement. For instance, when individual pieces are small—like pottery and glass flower frogs (top left)—more can be incorporated into a single display. You'll need fewer pieces if the items are large, like portrait heads (bottom left).

Don't insist on absolute precision with thematic groupings. Introduce a little chaos to produce a more spontaneous, natural look.

Colorful collections of red-and-white homespun or amber medicine bottles might add the only splash of color in an all-white room, but they can also inspire bold, complementary choices in curtains, upholstery, and carpets.

A collection's theme need not be confined to household goods alone. One collector who arranged orbs on a living room table (opposite) combined marble spheres with a gazing ball from the garden. A cast-iron urn filled with vintage croquet and boccie balls would make an equally eye-catching arrangement.

Large collections can be distributed throughout the house. If pugs are the objects of your affection, why not toss needlepoint pillows bearing images of the cuddly canines on the living-room sofa, have a pug doorstop in the kitchen, and group four-legged figurines on the bedroom dresser?

When your tastes range from classic country to the wonderfully wacky, achieving a cohesive look can be a challenge—and a lot of fun. Two homeowners chose a strong green for the living-room walls to ground their brightly hued collections. If the walls were white, individual pieces would stand out like large blotches of color. Clusters of similar objects—amateur oil portraits on the wall, a family of McCoy planters below the window, patterned pillows on the sofa—create concentrated areas of visual interest.

Folk Art

Although scholars endlessly debate the precise definition of folk art, in the flea market sense the term refers to the work of people who are untrained in the arts. Loosely interpreted, these objects can take any form—painting, sculpture, needlework. Folk art is often naïve in appearance and always charming in spirit.

Paintings are some of the most common forms of folk art found on the market. Common sightings range from oil-on-canvas still lifes and portraiture to inspired concoctions on plywood, masonite, and even on pieces of cardboard.

Keep an eye out for the work of undiscovered stars of the folk art world, who often sell early works in humble surroundings. Alabama painter Mose Tolliver, for instance, once arranged his housepaint-on-plywood creations on his front lawn and priced them at $1 apiece; now Tolliver's paintings hang in some of the nation's most prestigious galleries and museums.

Folk art garden sculpture is also sought after. Examples found at flea markets include wooden whirligigs and colorfully painted sheet-metal cutouts. Another popular category known as "whimseys" encompasses purely decorative objects like miniature figures carved from wood or soap and compositions of button art.

Because most folk art forms are one of a kind, determining value can be difficult. Age can affect an object's price, as can its color and quality of construction. The most important factor is whether the piece speaks to you.

When installing a particularly eye-catching object—like a sheet-metal shoe-store sign from the 1940s—keep the room's other furnishings as simple as possible (opposite). Many collectors purchase well-loved pedal cars at flea markets with the intention of restoring them to near-original condition. The owner of one 1930s tractor, on the other hand, chose to display his vintage treasure in all its weathered glory, turning the decades-old plaything into a work of art (right).

one-note collector

Confining a collection or an interior to a single color scheme gives a room a finished look with minimal fuss and draws attention to the intricacies of individual objects. All-white is one of the most popular interpretations of the look; here a large mirror, a shield-back side chair, and a creamware bowl peacefully coexist.

Signs

Old signs are hot commodities at flea markets around the country. Part of the popularity lies in the pure graphic appeal of the weathered pieces, but nostalgia also comes into play, for few items possess more obvious old-fashioned charm.

Although the technology to print on metal dates to the 19th century, tin signs became especially popular at least from the 1930s to the 50s. Wooden and enamel signs are harder to find.

Age affects the value of a sign. The earliest examples on the market are simply shapes—a large tooth outside the dentist's door, for example, or an oversized shoe above the shoemaker's shop—designed so that people who could not read would understand them.

Noncommercial, utilitarian signs such as "Back in Five Minutes," "Lunch Counter Closed," and our favorite, "GET BUSY!" are in high demand.

Signs for shop windows were most often lettered by professionals; hand-crafted ones are generally more valuable because they are one-of-a-kind.

Patriotic signs—"Uncle Sam Wants You!"—and those from the war decades—"Loose Lips Sink Ships!"—are extremely rare in their original forms. Reproductions are commonly available.

Because most signs were exposed to sun, wind, and rain on a regular basis, heavily worn surfaces are to be expected. Reproductions often imitate the appearance of wear and are usually a money-saving option for people in the market for a decorative accessory.

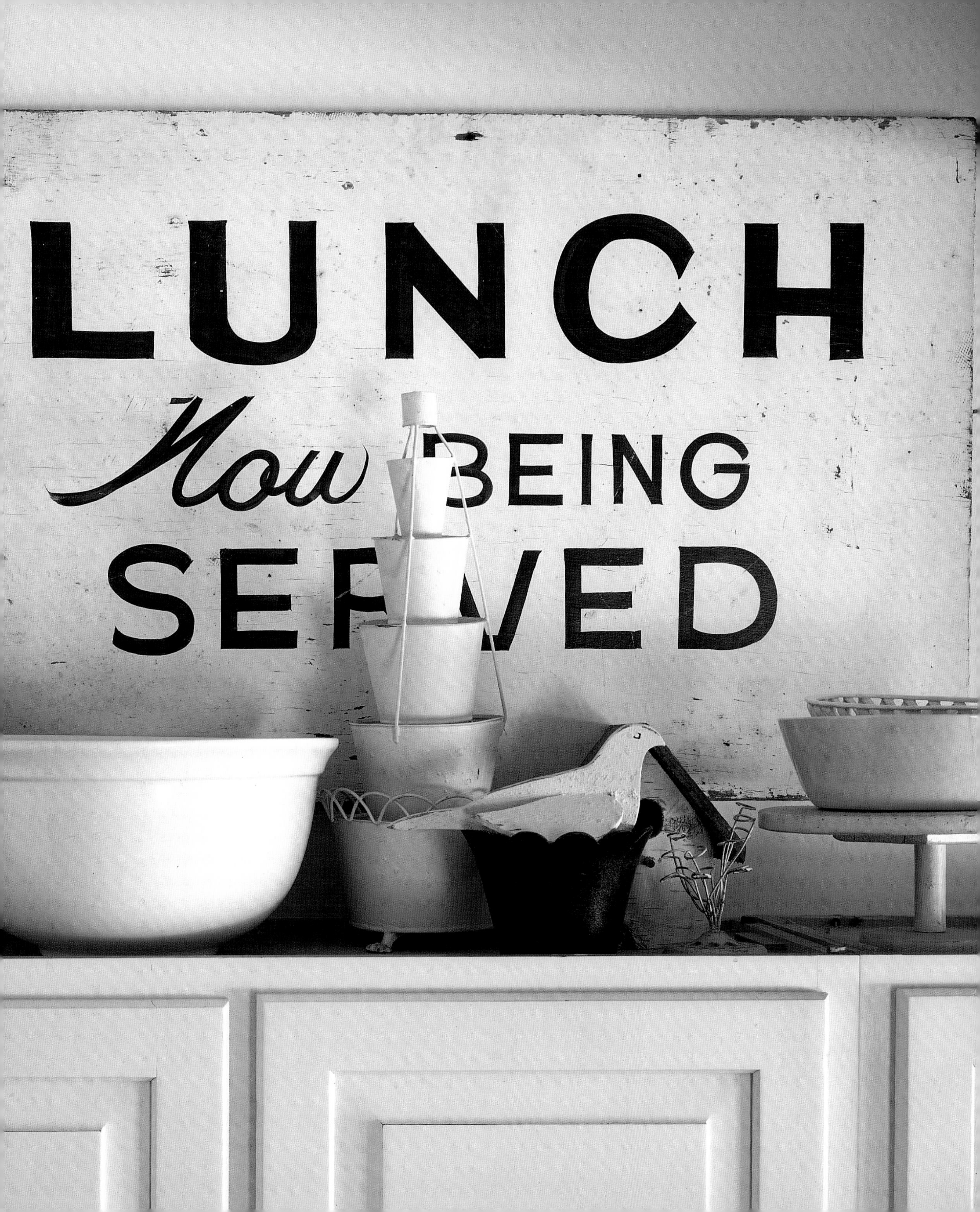
LUNCH
Now BEING
SERVED

Every inch of a light-filled dining room is imbued with the owner's love of flowers, from the furniture to the accessories to the artwork. The white frame of a large still life echoes the pattern of the Victorian architectural element beneath it; smaller artworks spread color throughout the space. An iron patio set from the 1950s is an unexpected—and delightful—furniture choice.

When decorating the dining room, don't feel limited to traditional furnishings. In lieu of the charcoal etchings and 19th-century-style portraits that commonly hang above an elegant sideboard, one adventurous couple mounted a 1920s kayak. Another homeowner took her silver flatware out of the drawer where it was ordinarily hidden away and grouped it in vases so the decorative handle designs could be enjoyed year-round.

How many times have you passed $1 stacks of mismatched dinner plates at a flea market? Choose a theme — a floral motif, perhaps, or green-and-white transferware patterns — and fill a cupboard with your inexpensive finds. Collections can even be incorporated into dinner-party table settings: Place a Jadeite eggcup with a single bloom at each seat, or set toy trains at the center of the children's table. Think seasonally too; put vases, garden pots, and urns to work, arranged with flowering branches in spring, cut flowers in summer, gourds in autumn, and evergreens wrapped with twinkly fairy lights in the winter.

A half dozen framed botanical prints hang in a row, echoing the long line of the dining room's pine farm table. Plates, glassware, and table linens are kept simple in suppertime arrangements: The superstar of this stage is a shimmering collection of beaded fruit, dramatically presented in a wire pedestal. Even the tomato-red side chairs echo the colors of the fabulous centerpiece.

flea market country

Rose Bowl Flea Market
Pasadena, California
Year-round

Silver

Although the majority of silver objects you'll see at flea markets today date from the mid-1900s, rare antiques do surface on occasion. Here are some hints for spotting treasures.

1. Invented in the eighteenth century, silver plate is created by adding a thin layer of silver over a base metal such as brass or copper. Common marks for newer silver include EPNS (for electroplated nickel silver), A1, and Quadruple Plate.

2. In most cases, sterling silver is more valuable than silver plate. Most sterling items made in the United States since the 1870s are marked with either "Sterling" or "925," which refers to a silver concentration of 925 parts per 1000.

3. To tell the difference between sterling and plate, study wear and tear. Plated wares sometimes reveal a blush of color from the base metal if they've been well-used or heavily polished. When the base metal is copper, some people refer to this wear as rosing, and admire the look.

4. Tarnish can also offer a clue. Sterling tends to tarnish to a warm grayish brown, while silver plate tarnishes to a cool black.

5. Because the base metals in silver plate are sometimes heavier than silver, a silver plate object may be heavier than a comparable sterling piece.

6. Silver plate is not always less expensive than sterling. Figural Victorian napkin rings are rarely sterling, but they are beautifully and intricately designed, and thus more costly.

7. An authoritative book of the hallmarks that appear on both sterling and silver plate is an invaluable addition to a collector's library. It will provide important information such as maker, date, and country of origin.

A parade of enamelware pitchers, filled with peonies, Queen Anne's lace, and hydrangeas marches along a painted bench in a rustic retreat (opposite). Because condition and pattern determine the value of enamelware, well-worn white pieces are affordable, plus they're easy to find. A pair of cattle portraits that once hung in the office of a dairy farmer and a 1950s hay rake reinforce the room's farmhouse feeling. On a tabletop (right), a soothing palette of soft blues and greens unifies disparate pieces.

grab it

A wooden screen door holds lots of potential in the home. Painted to match existing woodwork, a salvaged door can let light and air into a pantry while keeping flies out. Two or more doors hinged together create a folding screen for the bath; a light spray of white, gold, or silver paint gives the screen mesh a more delicate look.

Ironstone

The ceramic formula for ironstone was invented in England in 1813. Heralded as a more durable, more affordable alternative to the porcelain, bone china, and creamware of the day, ironstone enjoyed widespread popularity in both Europe and the United States from the 1840s to 1900.

While British families favored ironstone with colorful patterns, Americans generally preferred all-white designs, which explains why the majority of ironstone found at flea markets in the states today is pure white.

Patterns often reveal age. Early pieces displayed Gothic forms characterized by flattened hexagonal and octagonal panels. Embossed fruit, flowers, wheat, and other motifs were in vogue during the mid-1800s. Simple designs known as "farmer's china" were common toward the end of the century.

Some ironstone has brown staining where cracks in the outer glaze allowed the ceramic body to be exposed to the elements. These stains are really difficult to remove. Detergent is preferable to chlorine bleach, which is much too harsh.

Maker's marks range from elaborate logos with lions and unicorns to cryptic symbols inside diamond shapes, which refer to town of origin, pottery, and patent date. A reference guidebook will help you decipher these marks.

The graceful scalloped edges of ironstone cake stands flirt with the bold red shelves of a painted cupboard (right). Cake stands have unlimited versatility; a bounty of summer cherries is poised on a diminutive opaline design (opposite). A favorite trick of designers is creating a center-piece by stacking two or three stands on top of each other. For balance, smaller stands are placed on larger ones, and the display is filled out with fresh flowers, fruit, or holiday ornaments.

what to do?

Large collections do look lovely in the home, but even individual pieces can make an impact. A single beaded flower, for example, adds a whimsical touch to a traditional bouquet, while a beaded pear or banana tucked alongside the edible contents of a fruit bowl will likely bring a smile to someone's face.

Recreate a postwar kitchen by combining a typical table and chairs set with period table linens, glassware, and china (opposite). Red and yellow accents in a break-fast nook range from familiar kitchen accessories, like the red farm table and the yellowware jugs and bowls, to unexpected touches, like the antique game boards on a folk art shelf (right).

Once a strictly family domain, the kitchen has become a social space where folks gather to spend an hour or so before dinner, sipping a glass of wine and chatting with the cook. As a result, what may have seemed out of place in this room only a few years ago — comfortable armchairs, collections of pottery, even oil paintings — are now prominently displayed beside utilitarian canisters, ceramic mixing bowls, and enamel-topped tables.

As you stroll the aisles of a flea market, consider the rainbow that vintage kitchenware presents: the soft seashell pinks and buttery yellows of LuRay pastels, the saturated teals and reds of Fiestaware, the crisp apple-green of Depression glass, the muted moss-green of McCoy. Conversely, creamware and ironstone offer warm whites to soothe busy kitchen decors. Some homeowners echo the colors in window and wall treatments, while others allow the collections

A delicate wire basket filled with chirpy lemons and placed at a window (right) serves as a sunny welcome to guests as they approach the house. In a country kitchen, an amateur portrait from the 1940s adds a formal note (opposite). Mismatched seating around the table includes a late-1800s bowback side chair and a painted garden bench.

to take center stage by opting for an all-white background.

Larger kitchens benefit from collections, which can help to define space and separate work areas from comfort zones. Open shelves are a popular choice for many collectors; some remove the doors of existing cabinets to make room for stacks of plates and rows of pitchers. People who wish to showcase their cherished objects but are not terribly fond of dusting can get the best of both worlds with glass-front cupboards. A salvaged cupboard can house a collection, and it could be the inspiration for custom cupboards throughout the kitchen. If you are looking for a piece to help establish a separate area within the room, check the back panels of any cupboard you consider; a well-finished piece has more placement options.

flea market country

Piccadilly Antique & Collectible Fair
West Palm Beach, Florida
Year-round

Cupboards

Vintage cabinets bring instant charm to kitchens. Even if you find only a single attractive cupboard, make it part of your decor.

Appliances

Some folks outfit flea-market kitchens with refurbished appliances, but unobtrusive modern pieces focus attention on collections.

A Palette

Collections offer cheerful color, like the warming ochre of yellowware, the soft green of Jadeite, or the berry red of printed tablecloths.

Space to Eat
Plenty of comfortable seating is
one of the joys of the old-fashioned
country kitchen. A counter bar
invites lingering.

Light, Light, Light
Kitchens are welcoming when
flooded with daylight, but after sun-
down, light from vintage fixtures
complements collections.

Utensils
Kitchen items from the past
can still function in their original
manner. Stone crocks help keep
utensils within easy reach.

Wire whisks, strainers, and beaters frame a small kitchen window (right). Having such a specific object to search for at flea markets makes each outing a real treasure hunt; finding a design you've never seen before is a thrill. When displayed on countertops and along open shelves, kitchenware from the 1930s and '40s adds a sense of fun to modern rooms (opposite). Cookie jars and glass bottles serve as transparent storage for sweets, flour, pasta, pretzels, and other dry goods. Clusters of wood-handled utensils provide a punch of color.

what is it?

Before the days of hand-held mixers, mashed potatoes were made using a wooden masher with a flat bottom. The humble pieces display a surprising range of shapely silhouettes and, with few exceptions, are relatively inexpensive now. And they're still just as efficient mashing potatoes.

Gifts from the Sea

If you stop to consider that oceans, rivers, and lakes both refresh and sustain us, it should come as no surprise that Americans feel a close connection to imagery related to the seashore and the creatures that inhabit our many waterways. Vacation homes are especially appropriate places for these wares.

Among the items that can be discovered at flea markets today are sets of dinnerware including lobster-and-crab design from England and clear-glass lobster plates from Maine (opposite).

Some of the oldest, most valuable pieces are Victorian fish plates and platters (left). Popular from 1880 to 1900, they were originally sold in sets that included a large platter bearing the image of a salmon or trout along with 12 plates, each with a different species of fish on it.

As you might expect, hand-painted designs are more desirable than transfer-prints. Complete sets are rare, especially so in pristine condition.

English- and German-made porcelain with fish patterns is relatively easy to obtain. Because of its ocean trade and maritime culture, Japan has produced vast amounts of plates and serving dishes sporting fish and ocean life.

The most affordable items are souvenir glassware and plates from restaurants in areas like Cape Cod, Key West, and San Francisco.

Too Much?

An avid antiques collector tells the story of spotting an object at a flea market similar to one he already had at home. His shopping companion asked, "Do you really need that?" The collector's answer? "Need has nothing to do with it." Happily, there are solutions to the special decorating problems that arise from even the most outrageous case of have-to-have-it syndrome.

Custom-built shelves tame large collections. More than four hundred potato mashers line the shelves of one kitchen (opposite), while dozens of colorful cast-iron doorstops brighten a living-room bookcase (right).

Curio cabinets are practical, beautiful storage for fragile collections like Staffordshire figures or seashell crafts. Some cabinets found at flea markets lack their original glass doors. Luckily, doors can usually be replaced by a skilled carpenter, who will also wire the cabinet for interior lighting.

Display space should complement a collection. For example, glass ornaments glitter when placed in a spot that enjoys direct sunlight, while a row of vintage flowerpots is a natural partner for a weathered potting bench.

If you really run out of room, consider storing part of your collection and rotating the items on display several times a year. Always choose archival storage materials and select areas in the house where temperature and humidity fluctuations are minimal —attics and basements, therefore, are out.

Simple wooden shelves are a flea market staple. With careful placement in a narrow dressing area, they become charming, little display cases for collections like white McCoy pottery and amateur portraiture (right). In a garden-lover's bedroom, floral engravings and watercolors gathered over the years feel right at home (opposite). Vintage textiles were cut up to create the ruffled bed skirt and chair covers.

the bedroom is your sanctuary from the worries of the everyday world, so display here the pieces you love the most. An intimate grouping on a nightstand might include a vintage wind-up alarm clock, a silver bud vase, and a stack of 19th-century novels. An elegant dresser-top arrangement could feature vintage perfume bottles on a chintzware plate or a trio of milk-glass candy dishes that hold rings, keys, and change.

Before you begin a flea market search, you may already have a bedroom theme in mind — all white, perhaps, or something floral. Other times a decorating idea is sparked when you spot a single item, like a striking red-and-green quilt that demands green McCoy vases, redwork pillow shams, and a red painted rocker. When you're shopping, look beyond what we think of as conventional bedroom accessories to create your own personal style. A keen gardener, for example,

Even pared-down decorating styles benefit from a few well-chosen objects, like the vintage clocks, large letter, and silver teapot-turned-bud vase on a bedside table (opposite). Vanity accoutrements like Victorian ivorine shoe horns, cold cream jars, and manicure tools are a hit with collectors eager to recapture the grace of a more refined era (right).

might feed her passion for all things botanical. She could fashion a bed frame from a cast-iron fence, position a potting table and patio chair as a small desk set, and trail ivy on a trellis or a length of chicken wire around a window frame.

Ideas abound for children's rooms as well. Dress the bed with colorful quilts and fill a wall with paint-by-numbers pictures of ballerinas, horses, or clowns. Scoop up pegboards, which hold infinite possibilities for kids' room displays, like supporting a row of doll clothes suspended from tiny hangers. If you find a box of well-worn children's books, rifle through each volume to see if individual illustrations can be salvaged and framed. Open-shelf cupboards are also versatile; let them display doll collections, trophies, model rockets, and more. Encourage your kids to help in the hunt so flea market excursions become family outings; a satisfying first collection for kids is salt and pepper shakers.

A Dream Space

The first luxury is space: two smaller rooms can be combined to create one sunny interior. A low wall separates sleeping and dressing areas.

The Proper Bed

Let the bed frame complement the style of the room. The classic lines of a whitewashed design are well suited to a peaceful room.

Bedding Options

Linens should echo the style of the room. Chenille bedspreads, Depression-era quilts, and lace-trimmed shams are all popular.

Night Tables

A good night table comfortably accommodates a lamp, an alarm clock, and a vase for flowers. Shelves and drawers are a plus.

Closet Space

If existing closets are small, invest in an armoire or a cupboard that could have been transplanted from the kitchen or dining room.

A Few Favorite Things

Display your favorite collections and souvenirs. Vintage lingerie and christening outfits can be framed and hung on the walls.

Grace Notes

Elaborate displays have their place, but sometimes a single object or two can possess equal visual strength. Artful placement of these "grace notes" sparks smiles and invites quiet contemplation.

Viewed on its own instead of as part of a bouquet, a solitary stem trumpets the miracle of nature (opposite). A simple vase like a clear-glass medicine bottle focuses attention on the single bloom.

Diminutive paintings like a trio of oil-on-board seascapes (right) beckon the viewer to come closer. Charming wood frames call to mind the weather-worn buildings of a seaside town.

Mirrors reflect light, expand space, and double the impact of a visual gesture. Another graceful way to display a mirror is to hang it above a table with a broad, luxurious ribbon.

A lace doily brings an elegant finishing touch to a scene. Imagine, for example, a simple vase standing starkly on a bare mahogany dresser. Then visualize the same vase on a doily, like an angel on a cloud.

You may already have grace notes of your own, just waiting to be brought to life. Tie back sheer curtains with lengths of grosgrain ribbon, for instance, or stitch pearl buttons to the corners of a pillow sham.

Serenity reigns in an all-white bedroom, where an iron bed is dressed with inviting duvets and pillows. Wall lamps leave room on the nightstand for a large hydrangea bouquet, a bird's nest beneath an antique glass cloche, and a favorite snapshot in a shapely frame. Sheer curtains, a lace-edged linen tablecloth, and a whitewashed bistro chair add hints of texture throughout. The cross above the bed was crafted from scrap metal.

flea market country

Lakewood Antiques Market
Atlanta, Georgia
Year-round

A large built-in cupboard provides a luxury of space for bath necessities and collections (opposite). The juxtaposition of the delicate chandelier and a ladder-back rocking chair kindles visual interest in the spacious room. Throughout an unabashedly old-fashioned bathroom, framed engravings of seashells and marine life are the logical display (right).

baths present their own set of challenges to the flea market decorator. In bathrooms with very little surface space, walls become the main focus of attention. Images to look for include framed botanical prints, vintage seaside postcards, and Victorian advertisements for cold cream, talcum powder, and toilet water. A collection of mirrors hung on the wall would visually expand a small space. Antique hardware, such as coat hooks and towel racks, provide plenty of hands-on storage. To avoid confusion over whose towel is whose, locker room numbers can be hung from the hooks. You might consider installing shelves or positioning a standing medicine cabinet to hold favorite pieces like virtuous white art pottery or playful beach toys for a child's bath. Because humidity and splashing water pose a threat to vintage textiles, weathered wood, and unframed artwork, these collections are best on show in more accommodating areas of the home.

Milk glass and Jadeite bud vases are common finds at flea markets (opposite). Milk glass is a good deal less expensive, so one can build a sizeable collection quickly. When they are gathered together on a charming 1950s plant stand, the range of shapes, sizes, and patterns is apparent. Hard-milled soaps fill an enamelware basin set into an iron base (right). Openly storing the soaps allows their fragrance to permeate the room.

one-note collector

Green pottery is the special passion of many collectors. It is found in hundreds of shades, from emerald to teal to celadon to chartreuse. In such a collection, each piece enhances the tones of the others, and just two green ceramic pots together have a strong impact. Color collections are versatile enough to embrace high-ticket items as well as bargains.

Consider the impact collections can have in a room. In one bath, graphic panoramic photographs fill the wall from tub to ceiling, creating an amusing atmosphere that sparks countless thoughts and reminiscences (right). The accessories needed for a relaxing soak in the tub can be stored in attachable metal trays or simple side tables. For a peaceful setting more suited to contemplation, a single framed mirror provides the only ornamentation (opposite).

grab it

There are few furnishings as versatile as the country cupboard. Small wonder then that the pieces rarely spend much time in a dealer's booth before getting snatched up by a lucky shopper. In the dining room, grand stepback cupboards display heirloom china. Glass-front designs from the early 1900s work equally well in the kitchen, the bath, or any room in the house. Size, age, condition, and original finish can all affect a cupboard's price.

flea market forensics

You're at the gate to the flea market, but where do you begin? Some quickly tour the entire sale searching for special objects, then return to the starting point to methodically scour each booth. Others simply begin at the entry, carefully sifting through one dealer's space before moving on to the next. However you start, search each stand thoroughly. Unlike the orderly rows of products in retail stores, the jumble of a flea market stand is its appeal. Look to the sides, behind the dealer, under the table. It's a sale — you're allowed to open cartons and poke through stacks. Visualize how an item will look out of its current crowded setting. What about that vase filled with sweet peas and set on the mantel? Could a fresh coat of paint bring this dresser back to life? Feel free to ask the dealer to move other items so you can have a closer look.

If you love an item but it's highly priced, ask the dealer if he can do any better or offer an amount you'd be willing to pay.

Don't hesitate too long: A shopper can fall into a bargain mindset and lose an appreciation for what is really quite a bargain. A veteran once said "You only regret what you don't buy."

The Flea Market Shopper's Checklist

Some shoppers devote an entire Saturday or Sunday to flea marketing and leave their homes well-prepared for the challenge. But many fans keep a kit in their cars so that they'll be fully equipped for a spontaneous shopping adventure: Include —

- ✔ A cell phone and the numbers for knowledgeable friends you can call for advice.

- ✔ Swatches and color samples to see how items work together.

- ✔ A loupe and a magnifying glass, a tape measure and work gloves.

- ✔ The dimensions of the space and of your doorway, if you want a large piece to fit a spot in your home.

- ✔ An open mind and a little imagination—train yourself to see the possibilities in any given piece.

Country auctions If possible, always attend the auction preview, held a few days or a few hours before the sale. Inspect each lot, or item, up for sale closely; with few exceptions, purchases at auction are strictly "as is." Previews are a good time to decide upon a ceiling — a price above which you will not go — to avoid overpayment in a bidding war.

Choose a seat in full view of the auctioneer, front and center; if this area is full, stay within direct line of sight of the podium by moving to the back rather than to the side. When pieces you like come up for sale, join the bidding by holding your paddle or card straight up. After the initial flashing of your card, later bids can be made with a simple nod or raising of your hand. An inadvertent scratch of the nose will not result in an unintentional purchase; auctioneers know a real bid when they see one.

Yard sales All but the most impromptu yard sales are advertised in the local paper and on roadside signs. Even if the ad states that the sale starts at 8:00 a.m., serious collectors, antiques dealers, and decorators start lining up at the crack of dawn. Getting there early is the only way to beat the pros at their own game. Block sales, estate sales, and moving sales generally offer more and the incentive is greater for the seller to reduce prices.

thrift shops Thrift shops can be sources of terrific finds: They tend to do less research and be less aware of the value of really remarkable items. It's possible to stumble onto a beautiful old chair among all the ruined classroom desks and broken toys. Charity thrift stores get donations constantly, so the stock changes often. The key here is looking beyond the commonplace. The kitchenware section, for instance, may be a jumble of inexpensive florist vases and chipped juice glasses, but look closely: Sterling silver, fine china, and Fire-King are often hiding in the mix. Scour the bookshelves as well, for this area has been known to harbor collectible comic books, first editions, and autographed volumes. There is tremendous variety in the quality and character of thrift shops, so get to know your local stores and visit them often.

On-line auctions These auctions last anywhere from one week to one month. Devotees claim that there are two basic approaches to on-line bidding. The first is to decide your ceiling, bid that amount, and wait to hear, via email, if you win. Or you can follow the action right to the end of the sale and keep raising the stakes when you get outbid. The competition can become heated, so it's wise to set a ceiling, just as you would at a live auction.

Read the Terms and Conditions when you log onto a new site, as policies vary. Check the seller's feedback and deal only with people who have been consistently rated as honest. Contact a seller before bidding to ask about payment options, return policies, and any details of the item that may not be not visible in the photo.

Whatever its setting, any offering of formerly owned objects is likely to provide an exhilarating variety of pieces—bewildering to the beginner, exciting to the expert. Here are eighteen of the most common categories you'll encounter, with ways to gauge what is most valuable and what can be reinvented to suit a modern setting. Keep in mind that our labels are fluid, and that any attractive and functional object can be bent to a variety of uses—it can be cleaned, trimmed, refinished, restored, and totally reinvented.

Advertising

Just about anything that has been emblazoned with a manufacturer's logo falls into this category. Among the numerous types you'll find on the market are calendars, measuring-tape cases, match holders, bookmarks, letter openers, paperweights, shoehorns, thermometers, ashtrays, and piggy banks. Kitchens are common places to display items like tin canisters, serving trays, and salt & pepper shakers (especially fine collections for beginners). Some people search for old magazine ads and store displays that relate to popular name-brand collections like Fiestaware, Fire-King, and LuRay pastels. Brand names rendered in ceramic, like Roseville and Rolling Rock, are rare and very valuable.

Americana

American antiques have a sincerity and a simplicity lacking in contemporary, mass-produced patriotic objects. A well-placed Uncle Sam bank or a flag with fewer than fifty stars is an appealing and personal way to express your allegiance. Americana is, in fact, extraordinarily large in scope: vintage prints of presidents and historic events, dolls and old signs, campaign buttons and military medals. Make sure that flags are displayed correctly—stars should always be in the upper left corner with a single, constant source of illumination at night—as per the Flag Code of 1924. The code itself is highly collectible, as are scout guides on flag etiquette, schoolhouse watercolors of George Washington, and framed photographs of more recent presidents.

one-note collectors

"One-note" collectors know that there is beauty in the object and joy in numbers.

- tin florist vases
- hat stands
- white vases
- flower frogs

- game boards
- cameras
- perfume bottles
- Jadeite

Architectural Salvage

Common sightings include old doors, windows, floorboards, mantels, shutters, tin ceiling panels, balusters, newel posts, millwork, bathroom tiles, marble sinks, and claw-foot tubs. Owing to crossover demand from both home restorers and antiques collectors, expect to pay more for objects that can stand on their own artistically, like a leaded- or stained-glass window or an ornate section of wrought-iron fencing. If you're searching for a mantel, door, or decorative detail to complement the architecture of your home, consult design books to identify common motifs you can look for at flea markets and salvage shops.

just as good

Although cleaning or rewiring may be called for, many vintage objects still work as they were originally intended.

- electric fans
- toasters
- lighting
- vacuum cleaners
- juicers
- typewriters
- turntables
- kitchen clocks

Art & Photography

Paintings, prints, and photographs are the most common art found at flea markets. The majority of paintings are amateur still lifes, landscapes, and portraits of people and pets. Paint-by-numbers have become quite popular with collectors of kitsch, who cluster the playful images in groups. Victorian tintypes can be found by the boxful and incorporated into tabletop arrangements; some black-and-white landscape and still life photographs look quite beautiful framed. Prints range from commercial offerings like Currier & Ives images to limited-edition art prints. Look for the artist's signature in pencil beneath the image in the lower right corner; on the lower left are the quantity of the printing and the number of your print. The lower your number, the higher the value.

Baskets

Fashioned from willow branches, hickory splints, sweet grass, and rye straw, baskets have been made for every conceivable chore—toting laundry, storing sewing supplies, and carrying eggs, herbs, flowers, and fruit. Vintage pieces are good for both display and utilitarian purposes, while inexpensive new designs are often scooped up for gift-giving. Native American baskets have a strong following among collectors, but examples predating the 1940s have become increasingly rare. Connoisseurs have been known to supplement their

grab it

Certain objects are coveted by certain collectors, but some items are appreciated by all who view them.

- kids' watering cans
- folding screens
- painted cupboards
- schoolhouse memorabilia
- French enamelware
- vintage luggage
- linen sheets
- patio furniture

collections with handsome new creations that have been made in the traditional manner by tribes living in Maine, the Upper Midwest, and the Southwest, where they sometimes set up tables at local flea markets. An added benefit of these baskets is that because of their provenance, they'll likely increase in value.

Books

Books abound at flea markets. While some can be quite rare—antiquarian first editions or large art volumes— most are inexpensive and appropriate for decorative displays throughout the house. A pile of garden books from the 1930s and '40s can be a wonderful addition to a sun room, while a row of detective fiction in a guest room will give overnight visitors a choice of literature. View the reds, greens, and warm browns of old book spines as opportunities to add a dash of color to a setting. One creative homeowner removed botanical illustrations from their binding and had them framed.

Ceramics

Although earlier wares do appear at flea markets from time to time, the oldest ceramics you're likely to see today are yellowware bowls and ironstone dinnerware from the early 1900s. The most common art pottery you'll spot are the mass-produced, mid-20th-century lines from potteries like Haeger, Roseville, Shawnee, Hull, Weller, Rookwood, and Van Briggle. In fact, it's an odd flea market that doesn't

offer at least a half dozen pots. Some pieces are purely decorative, but vases, planters, and bowls can hold pencils and scissors at the office, spools of thread and yarn in the sewing room, and soaps and washcloths in the bath. Bulb pots are still perfect for forcing flowering bulbs. If you are seduced by pottery, and countless people have been, refer to specialty art pottery books that are devoted to single manufacturers, and follow online auctions to keep current with valuations. Those wares intended for kitchen duty, such as Russel Wright, Bauer, and Fiesta, are as beautiful and functional as ever. It's best not to serve food in art pottery, or to place it in a dishwasher. To narrow their search, many people focus on a single manufacturer, a color, a motif, or a design (cookie jars, flowerpots, wall pockets). Without a doubt, the best hunting ground for ceramics is the Pottery Week in Zanesville, Ohio, an event that is held one week each July.

Ephemera

Ephemera is an umbrella term used to describe objects that were not intended to be saved, like ticket stubs, dance cards, receipts, and campaign flyers. At first glance, much of the material found on the market seems to hold more historical value than decorative potential. Once they are framed, however, many of the items can be displayed around the house, like graphic diner menus in the kitchen, colorful seed catalogs in the garden room, dress-pattern packaging in the sewing room, and vintage *Life* magazine covers in the den. Greeting cards—especially penny Valentines from the 1930s and '40s—are also popular as holiday decorations.

sporting equipment

No doubt about it, America is a land of sports lovers, evident in the breadth of theme collectibles on the market.

- cheerleading
- croquet
- bowling
- birdwatching

- darts
- shuffleboard
- fishing
- badminton

Fashion

Vintage fashions have become so popular in the past few years that even Hollywood stars don them while sashaying along red carpets. In addition to being worn, these items can serve in countless ways around the house. Hang flowery Easter bonnets in an arc around an elegant vanity mirror, for instance; frame 1950s bowling shirts and old-fashioned team uniforms and arrange them with other sports memorabilia in a playroom or den. Long-outgrown children's clothing is also in demand; imagine an adorable calico dress, a diminutive straw hat, or several pairs of tiny woolen mittens hanging from a pegboard in a girl's room.

Folk Art

Naïve paintings, sculptures, and textile creations are the pieces spotted most often in this category. Many homeowners incorporate folk art into decidedly country settings—mounting weather vanes above the mantel or positioning a hooked rug in front of the hearth. Other collectors elevate a single piece of folk art to fine art by mounting a humble painting in an ornate gilded frame or placing a sheet metal

sculpture on an elegant pedestal. Rustic birdhouses and handmade dollhouses are some of the most eagerly sought forms of folk art; one wonderful piece should be the focal point of a room.

Garden Ornaments

These days, anything that was originally intended for the garden is welcome indoors, so expect to see old tools, porch chairs, lawn ornaments, and birdhouses just about everywhere you look. A weathered wheel-

barrow, an ornate cast-iron bench, and a painted wood trellis—all have innate beauty whether they're indoors or out. Repurposing serves some garden items, like positioning a painted garden bench as a coffee table in front of the sofa, or setting a tiny watering can filled with paint brushes and colored pencils on a worktable.

Glass

Glass manufacturing on a grand scale began in the United States in the 19th century and produced so many shapes, patterns, sizes, and colors that all but the rarest examples are modestly priced. The most abundant styles date to the Depression, when milk glass, Jadeite, and the familiar shades of pink, green, cobalt, and amber glass were produced by the trainload. As you examine a piece, lightly run your finger around the top and base to check for tiny cracks; hold it up to the light to look for hairline cracks. When arranging glass, consider the light source: Windowsills, glass cabinets beside windows, and built-in glass shelves against a window all allow day-light to enhance the translucent quality of glass; tiny spotlights are effective after dark.

Kitchenware

Whether one's goal is to re-create a Postwar American kitchen or simply to add to a collection of salt & pepper shakers, flea markets over-flow with clever, functional kitchenware. There are choices for country kitchens (enamel-topped tables, printed cotton tablecloths, old-fashioned scales, wire whisks) and modern kitchens as well (Art Deco chrome tea sets, futuristic plastic dinnerware from the 1950s,

Pyrex mixing bowls, and refrigerator containers in typical 1960s colors like mustard and avocado). The joy of kitchen collectibles is that they are as useful today as they were decades ago.

farm tools

Part of America's heritage, agricultural artifacts are eagerly sought by collectors and decorators alike.

- pitchforks
- rakes
- ladders
- yokes
- scythes
- field baskets
- pruning shears
- wheelbarrows

Metal

All kinds of household items crafted from silver, brass, copper, pewter, aluminum, and other metals can be found at a flea market. Serious collectors often arrive armed with price guides, searching to uncover the rarity among the boxes and boxes filled with silver-plate teaspoons. Professional designers are really more interested in an object's display potential in the home. Decorate a mantel with brass candlesticks of all shapes and sizes, fill a silver fruit bowl with ornate silver napkin rings, line the shelves of a step-back cupboard with pewter chargers, or cover a kitchen wall with jelly molds and copper pans. The surfaces of copper and tin pots can be restored for far less than the cost of new pots. Vintage hardware—door hinges, window locks, and drawer pulls—still work superbly (though they may need to have generations of paint removed first).

flea classics

You're sure to spot these flea-market staples at sales from Portland, Maine, to Portland, Oregon, and everywhere in between.

- Bakelite utensils
- Depression glass
- McCoy pottery
- ironstone
- printed tablecloths
- canning jars
- trade signs
- iron bed frames

Notions

Button tins, bottle cap collections, rubber-band balls—objects that don't seem to fit into a traditional collecting category are known as notions. Single objects (perhaps an elaborate popsicle-stick house, a make-do pincushion, or a seashell-encrusted dresser box) placed either alone or in an arrangement often spark spirited conversations among guests. Notions are also snatched up at flea markets by creative folks who transform snippets of velvet dress trimming, buttons, baubles, and beads into one-of-a-kind crafts. And because serious collectors often overlook these humble items, they are rarely expensive, allowing shoppers to purchase the whimsical pieces on a whim.

Primitive **F**urniture

For years now, furniture displaying simple lines and a handcrafted look has been a hot seller. Painted finishes are particularly popular; dealers report that blue and white pieces sell the fastest, with red and green items coming in close behind. Because 19th-century furnishings have become scarce, expect most cupboards, pie chests, dry sinks, and farm tables you spot today to date from around 1900 to 1930. Be wary of painted finishes that have a uniform pattern of wear, as this may be a sign of recent manufacture. Authentic pieces often display deep crackling in the paint and concentrated wear around door handles and drawer pulls. In addition to serving as a sign of authenticity, this evidence of long and loving use gives any piece a warmth and charm that will enrich the room around it.

Textiles

Tables filled with vintage textiles never fail to attract a crowd at flea markets. Quilts are perennial favorites, but as prices for antiques continue to rise, today's homeowners look to examples from the 1940s and '50s to build colorful collections. Quilt tops and individual blocks are inexpensive alternatives to completed antique quilts as well; frame a series of quilt blocks for an eye-catching

wall display. Building a new quilt from blocks of old quilts enables you to flex your creativity while re-creating antiques to suit the design of your own individual room. Household linens like tablecloths, napkins, and tea towels are also in steady demand, as are remnants of mid-20th-century upholstery fabric, which can be used for slipcovers, clothing, and crafts, depending on how much yardage is available in a particular pattern.

holidays

Commonly seen objects include not only decorations but also greeting cards, paper plates, figural candles, and the like.

- Christmas
- New Year's Eve
- Valentine's Day
- St. Patrick's Day
- Easter
- Independence Day
- Halloween
- Thanksgiving

Toys

Although action figures and fashion dolls from the past quarter century have become flea market staples, there are literally thousands of playthings from the early to mid-1900s that have an older, more naïve style appreciated by collectors. Arrange graphic board games on a playroom wall, or line a mantel or bookshelf with colorful tin wind-up toys. Metal mechanical banks shaped like people, manufactured between 1900 and 1930, are also popular—place a coin in its hand, pull a lever, and the bank pops the coin into its mouth. A formation of real tin soldiers will balance out a silverware set or a pair of brass candlesticks, showing off the unique finish and wear of each. For an unexpected display, group small items like alphabet blocks or mah-jongg tiles in bowls or tins. Keep an eye out for robot toys from the 1950s and '60s, which number among the hottest commodities with collectors, but be wary of reproductions, which often feature gleaming, unblemished finishes.

photography credits

Jim Bastardo
Pages 16, 25, 162

Pascal Blancon
Page 79

Pierre Chanteau
Pages 7 (top row, second), 18 (top right), 28, 29, 170 (left)

Philip Clayton-Thompson
Page 120 (bottom)

Roger Cook
Pages 140 (bottom), 144

Jonn Coolidge
Pages 1 (bottom left), 7 (bottom row, fourth), 37, 38, 39, 73, 84–85, 88, 89, 90

Grey Crawford
Pages 6 (top row, third), 55, 112

Kate Gatsby
Page 132 (bottom)

Gridley & Graves
Pages 31, 40, 65 (right), 102, 132 (top), 133, 148, 169 (top right and bottom right)

Steve Gross & Sue Daley
Pages 2, 6 (top row, second), 6 (bottom row, third), 7 (top row, third), 18 (bottom right), 24 (top), 52 (top), 53, 58 (bottom), 60–61, 64, 80, 98 (top left), 119 (top), 130, 131, 137, 154–155, 160 (bottom), 167 (left), 168 (right), 170 (bottom right), 173 (right)

Mark Lohman
Pages 6 (bottom row, fifth), 30 (top right)

Michael Luppino
Page 75

Steven Mays
Pages 9, 59, 142

Andrew McCaul
Pages 6 (top row, first), 18 (bottom left), 34, 35, 41, 78 (bottom), 87 (right), 173 (bottom left)

Jeff McNamara
Pages 6 (top row, fifth), 172 (top right)

Keith Scott Morton
Pages 1 (bottom right), 4–5, 6 (top row, fourth), 7 (top row, fourth), 7 (bottom row, first), 7 (bottom row, fifth), 15, 20, 22–23, 26–27, 36, 42, 44 (top left), 46–47, 48, 49, 50–51, 54, 56–57, 58 (top), 62, 63, 66–67, 68, 69, 70 (right), 71, 74, 76–77, 78 (top), 82, 87 (left), 91, 92–93, 95 (top), 96, 98 (top right and bottom right), 101, 106, 108–109, 110 (top), 111, 113, 114–115, 118, 119 (bottom), 120 (top), 123, 124–125, 126–127, 128, 129 (top), 134, 136, 140 (top), 143, 146, 147, 149, 150–151, 152, 153, 156, 158, 159 (bottom), 160 (top), 161, 171 (top right and bottom right), 172 (bottom right)

Helen Norman
Pages 6 (bottom row, first), 44 (bottom left), 86

David Prince
Pages 1 (top left), 7 (top row, fifth), 7 (bottom row, second), 10, 44 (top right), 52 (bottom), 65 (left), 104–105, 121, 168 (bottom left), 170 (top right)

Steven Randazzo
Pages 1 (top right), 6 (bottom row, second), 24 (bottom), 44 (bottom right), 70 (left), 103 (top), 110 (bottom), 116, 117, 145, 157, 159 (top)

Jeremy Samuelson
Pages 32, 98 (bottom left)

William P. Steele
Pages 19, 129 (bottom)

Cheryl Ungar
Pages 6 (bottom row, fourth), 171 (left), 173 (top left), 176

Dominique Vorillon
Pages 7 (top row, first), 18 (top left), 21

Jessie Walker
Pages 7 (bottom row, third), 33, 81, 83, 94, 135, 138–139, 141, 170 (middle right), 171 (middle right), 172 (left)

Paul Whicheloe
Pages 95 (bottom), 103 (bottom), 167 (bottom right), 168 (top left), 169 (left)

CASE PHOTOGRAPHY CREDITS

Front, clockwise from top left:
David Prince
Keith Scott Morton
Keith Scott Morton
Jonn Coolidge
Steven Randazzo

Spine:
Pierre Chanteau

Back, left to right:
Cheryl Ungar
Jeff McNamara
Keith Scott Morton